The Asymmetric PTSD Scale

Thomas Hodge

AS-PTSD Scale

Over the past few decades, Post-Traumatic Stress Disorder (PTSD) has received a great deal of attention due to recent publicity and awareness regarding the disorder. There have been a number of measures and methods that attempt to determine the presence of PTSD. PTSD is identified by the individual experiencing a traumatic event, re-experiencing the traumatic event through triggers, avoiding the triggers, and physiological arousal as a result of the experience (American Psychiatric Association, 2000). PTSD has drawn much attention as a result of veterans of wars returning from combat with the signs and symptoms of the disorder. Many of the individuals suffering from PTSD have avoided treatment due to stigma associated with the condition among military communities throughout the years. Due to the stigma associated with the condition, early screening and detection of PTSD has become important in acquiring treatment for the disorder (Hagsma et. al. , 2012).

Several measures have been created to evaluate the presence of PTSD symptoms in individuals. Those measures include the Impact Event Scale (IES-R), the Watson PTSD interview (PTSD-I), and the Mississippi Combat Related Scale (M-PTSD). These three measures serve as the most commonly used measures that focus on PTSD in combat veterans. The measures have found to be highly correlated with correlations ranging from .883 to .906

(Ljubotia & Muslic, 2003). Among these scales, the M-PTSD has been one of the most commonly used measures of PTSD in combat veterans. The M-PTSD has had several variations over the years and alternate forms. There are versions for both civilian and military populations. The M-PTSD Scale for Combat-Related PTSD consists of 35 questions that the symptoms of PTSD by self-reported responses. The M-PTSD utilizes a five-point scale that is similar to the Likert Scale for responses to items. The M-PTSD was designed to measure the presence of the symptoms of Post-Traumatic Stress Disorder based on the criteria provided in the *DSM-IV-TR*. The scale focuses on the presence of re-experiencing behaviors, hyperarousal, depression, and substance abuse (Keane, Caddell, & Taylor, 1998).

The M-PTSD can be administered in a brief period of time. Typically, the test can be completed in ten to fifteen minutes. The M-PTSD is scored by reversing the responses on positively worded items and adding up the responses to all of the questions. The M-PTSD utilizes a cut-off score of 121 to determine if the individual is suffering from PTSD. Originally, the cut-off score was 107, but it was found that such a low score was producing a high number of false positives for PTSD diagnoses as the mean score among veterans was 104.5 with a standard deviation of 26.2 (Keane, Caddell, & Taylor, 1988). Among college undergraduates, Lauterbach, Vrana, King, and King (1997) found of 73.5 and 74.4 to be consistent.

The M-PTSD has been shown to have strong reliability and validity. The M-PTSD does possess high levels of reliability with a test-retest of .97 and an internal consistency of .94 (Keane, Caddell, & Taylor, 1988). Cook et. al. (2005) found the M-PTSD to be significantly correlated with the PTSD Checklist scale (PCL), which serves a standard existing measure of PTSD symptoms. With the change of the cut-off score to 121, the M-PTSD has shown high levels of sensitivity (.95), but a low level of specificity (.45) (Lyons, Caddell, Pittman, Rawls, & Perrin, 1994). With such low levels of specificity, one could misinterpret the results of the M-PTSD as indicating the presence of Post-Traumatic Stress Disorder symptoms when actually a different condition may be present.

The M-PTSD was developed in the late 1980s. Over time one can notice that the validity of the test may be seen as declining due to cultural and generational changes in the populations over the years. Due to several policy changes and military practices, the manner in which military members perceive their experiences have changed. With such changes the M-PTSD's levels of validity may have changed and an update the measure would be needed to maintain the ability of the measure to detect the presence of PTSD symptoms early and discern such symptoms from other conditions and disorders. Cook et. al.

(2005) found that the M-PTSD was effective in screening for PTSD symptoms in elderly individuals as the symptoms are often overlooked due to the symptoms being mistaken for cognitive decline presented as the result of dementia or psychosis. The M-PTSD has shown high levels of success in screening older individuals for PTSD signs and symptoms as compared to clinical evaluations that tend to confabulate Post-Traumatic Stress Disorder with Dementia.

Keane, Caddell, and Taylor (1988) presented the M-PTSD as a measure of PTSD symptoms in Vietnam-era veterans suffering from the disorder. Over the twenty-five years since the development of the M-PTSD, generational changes have affected the mindset of service members and changes in the combat environment have also produced differences in the traumas experienced by veterans of the more current wars. As the perceptions of the individuals suffering from the disorder have changed along with the society as a whole, changes to the way in which the symptoms are evaluated should be assessed to address such changes. The M-PTSD focuses on the presence of anger arousal and the exposure of the individual to life-threatening situations based on the perceptions of the era in which it was created. On the modern-day battlefield, those stressors have changed due to the changes in the style of combat that is experienced. Vietnam-era veterans experience a more traditional combat experience with symmetrical lines of confrontation between opposing forces. During Operation Iraqi Freedom (OIF) and Operation Enduring Freedom (OEF), the opposing forces and division of forces was blurred and indiscernible in many cases. As the model of combat has changed, the development of symptoms and presentation of such symptoms have changed as a result of differing perceptions of what is seen as life-threatening situations.

In considering the social, cultural, and combat-related changes that have occurred since the development of the M-PTSD, new measures may be more effective in discriminating the symptoms of PTSD from other disorders and behaviors that are present among modern service members who have had different experiences in Iraq and Afghanistan as opposed to the Vietnam-era veterans. The Asymmetric Post-Traumatic Stress Disorder Scale (AS-PTSD) was designed to address such concerns as the changes in PTSD symptomology as a result of change from symmetrical, or traditional, warfare to asymmetrical, or non-traditional, warfare that is based on the complex changes resulting in confusion about who are and are not combatants.

The AS-PTSD will be normed by using a representative sample of veterans diagnosed with PTSD, veterans determined to not have PTSD, and Civilians not determined to have PTSD. The AS-PTSD will be normed through a study of 300 individuals with one-third being PTSD-diagnosed veterans, one third being non-

PTSD veterans, and one-third being non-PTSD civilians to determine the most effective cut-off score to diagnosis PTSD. To determine a normed cut-off score, the results would be examined to find the means and standard deviation of the norming group. The score that would coincide with one and a half standard deviations above the mean for the norming group would serve as the cut-off score for a diagnosis of PTSD. This study proposes that the AS-PTSD scale will provide levels of reliability and validity in assessing OIF/OEF veterans similar to the high levels of reliability and validity that the M-PTSD did in assessing Vietnam-era veterans.

Methods

Participants

PTSD veterans will consist of 100 OIF/OEF veterans that have been diagnosed with PTSD from the Huntington, West Virginia, Veterans Affairs Hospital. Non-PTSD veterans will consist of 100 OIF/OEF veterans that have been screened for PTSD and been determined not have PTSD from the Huntington, West Virginia, Veterans Affairs Hospital. Non-PTSD civilians will consist of 100 undergraduate students from Introductory Psychology courses at Marshall University that have been screened for PTSD and determined not to have PTSD. The PTSD and non-PTSD veterans will be given the measure voluntarily during routine checkups. The non-PTSD civilians will be given course credit for participation in the study. The PTSD and non-PTSD veterans will be selected by providing the first 100 veterans with PTSD and first 100 veterans without PTSD with the scales during routine checkups. The scales will continue to be presented to each group until 100 veterans of each group have completed the measure. The civilian sample will be a convenience sample of 100 undergraduate students from four different Introductory Psychology classes at Marshall University with 25 students from each class.

Materials

Paper copies of the AS-PTSD and the M-PTSD for each participant will be used along with a set of instructions for each participant. Each participant will use number two pencils to fill out the scales and a blue ink pen to sign the informed consent form.

The AS-PTSD will be consist of 25 statements that require a response on a Likert Scale that ranges from 1 to 7 with 1 representing "not at all" and 7 representing "all the time". The M-PTSD would consist of a 5-point, Likert style response questionnaire with 35 items. Written informed consent forms will be provided to each participant with a carbon copy attached of the informed consent also attached. A table and chair will be provided to use for the PTSD and non-PTSD veterans to use for filling out the M-PTSD and AS-PTSD scales. The civilian participants will use desks in Harris Hall room 231 on Marshall University's Huntington campus.

Procedure

The PTSD veterans will be presented

with the option of completing the questionnaires at the end of a routine check-up. The attending physician will be briefed prior to presentation of the scales. The physician will ask if the veteran would like to complete a survey to help determine the presence of PTSD in newly returning veterans. If the veteran agrees to complete the questionnaires, he will be presented with the informed consent that will be signed by the veteran and the physician once the physician has verbally reviewed the informed consent with the veteran. The veteran and physician will both sign with a blue ink pen. Upon completion of the informed consent, fifty of the PTSD and fifty of the non-PTSD veterans will be presented with the AS-PTSD first. The other half of the PTSD and non-PTSD groups will be presented with the M-PTSD first to counterbalance the order of test presentations. Upon receiving the measure, the veteran will be informed to write a "V+" in the upper right-hand corner of the test if the veteran has experienced PTSD symptoms. If the veteran has not been diagnosed with PTSD, the veteran will write "V-" in the upper right hand corner to determine whether a participant with or without PTSD took the test. The physician will informed the participant that the questionnaire is usually completed in five to ten minutes, but the participant can take as long as needed to complete the measure. The physician will inform the

Upon completing the first scale, the

participant will give the physician the questionnaire. The physician will then provide the patient the second questionnaire to complete. The second measure will be presented to the veteran immediately after they have completed the first measure. The veteran would be informed to complete the second questionnaire in the same manner as the first using the same number two pencil. After completing the second questionnaire, the participant will give the physician the completed questionnaire. The physician will then debrief the participant, and the participant will be free to leave.

The civilian non-PTSD participants will be given the measure during Introductory Psychology courses at Marshall University. At the beginning of their class, they will be presented with the informed consent by the researcher. The researcher will verbally review the informed consent and answer any questions that the participants may have prior to administering the questionnaires. The researcher will inform the classes that the questionnaires will each take ten to fifteen minutes to complete and will then distribute the first questionnaire to the participants along with number two pencils. Two of the classes will be presented with the M-PTSD first. The other two classes will be presented with the AS-PTSD first. Upon completion of all questionnaires, the researcher will tell the participants to pass the completed forms to the front of the class for collection. Once the questionnaires are collected, the researcher will distribute the second questionnaire to the participants. The researcher will inform the students that the second questionnaire normally takes ten to fifteen minutes to complete also. Once all questionnaires have been distributed, the researcher will tell the participants to begin the questionnaires. Once all the participants have completed the second questionnaire, the researcher will tell them to pass the questionnaires to the front of the class for collection. The researchers will then debrief the participants, and the participants will continue with the remainder of their class.

Statistics

After collecting the data, the AS-PTSD will be examined for reliability by using the split-half technique to determine the level of reliability in the instrument. The validity of the measure will be examined by examining the convergent validity with the M-PTSD. The prediction of the test will be compared to the actual presence of a PTSD diagnosis by use of the phi coefficient to determine how accurately the AS-PTSD accurately determines the diagnosis of PTSD. For the purpose of norming, a score of 1.5 standard deviations above the mean across all groups will serve as the cut-off score for determining the presence of PTSD on the AS-PTSD scale.

Conclusion

The AS-PTSD attempts to address generational changes that have developed since the advent of the M-PTSD and changes in combat environments, which are the catalysts that create the trauma. The measure does well in attempting to address this changes and new dynamics that individuals are more aware of in combat scenarios than they were during the Vietnam Era that was influential was the time period in which the M-PTSD was created. The need for early screening and detection of PTSD is essential due to the recent conflicts in the Middle East and Afghanistan.

With the development of future measures, research should focus on the early signs that predict chronic issues occurring. Many measures focus on the symptomology that occurs in the later stages of PTSD development. To more effectively develop early screening, longitudinal qualitative studies of returning veterans should be conducted to identify early factors and symptoms with following quantitative meta-analysis of the observations to determine significant factors in the development of PTSD during early stages of the disorder.

Appendix A

Asymmetric Post-Traumatic Stress Disorder Questionnaire

Rate the statements about life since your return from deployment using the following scale:

1.   Not at all

2.   Happened once

3.   Rarely happened

4.   Happens half of the time

5.   Happens the majority of the time

6.   Very rare not to happen

7.   All the time

1. I am easily startled in public.

_____

2. I feel uneasy in strange situations.

_____

3. I always make sure no one is behind me.

_____

4. Strange people make me nervous.

_____

5. I have difficulty concentrating.

_____

6. I find myself avoiding friends and family.

_____

7. Relaxing situations seem to be more stressful.

_____

8. I feel depressed.

_____

9. I have panic attacks.

_____

10. I have nightmares that feel very real.

_____

11. I have problems sleeping.

_____

12. I find myself avoiding situations that remind me about my deployment.

_____

13. I feel like I cannot change the way I feel.

_____

14. I feel like I need to try to control every-thing.

_____

15. I engage in behaviors that other say are dangerous.

_____

16. I get upset with others easily.

_____

17. I wake up from sleep in a panic.

_____

18. I drink alcohol to feel better about my life.

_____

19. I have mood swings.

_____

20. I find it difficult to trust friends and family.

_____

21. I feel like I do not have any energy.

_____

22. I do not like to talk about how I feel to others.

_____

23. I have trouble completing tasks.

_____

24. I find myself obsessing about little details.

_____

25. I feel like I am in a dangerous situation.

_____

To score sum the responses, based on a norming group a score of 1.5 standard deviations about the mean of the norming group serves as a cut-off score once the scores have been referenced to a large sample. Prior to the norming process, the following scale is used to determine the likelihood of PTSD symptomology.

Absence of PTSD- 25 to 55

Low likelihood of PTSD- 56 to 95

Moderate likelihood of PTSD- 96 to 140

High Likelihood of PTSD- 141-175

References

Cook, J. M., Elhai, J. D., Cassidy, E. L., Ruzek, J. I.,

Ram, G., & Sheikh, J. I. (2005). Assessment of Trauma Exposure and Post-Traumatic Stress in Long-Term Care Veterans: Preliminary Data on Psychometrics and Post-Traumatic Stress Disorder Prevalence. *Military Medicine, 170*(10), 862-866.

Haagsma, J., Ringburg, A., van Lieshout, E., van Beeck, E., Patka, P., Schipper, I., & Polinder, S. (2012). Prevalence rate, predictors and long-term course of probable posttraumatic stress disorder after major trauma: a prospective cohort study. *BMC Psychiatry, 12*(1), 236-244. doi:10.1186/1471-2393-12-236.

Keane, T. M., Caddell. J. M.. & Taylor, K. L. (1988). Mississippi Scale for CombatRelated Posttraumatic Stress Disorder: Three studies in reliability and validity. *Journal of Consulting and Clinical'Psychology.*56,85-90.

Lauterbach, D., Vrana, *S.,* King, D. W., & King, L. A. (1997). Psychometric properties of the civilian version of the Mississippi PTSD Scale. *Journal of Traumatic Stress, 10,* 499-513.

Ljubotina, D., & Muslić, L. (2003). Convergent validity
of four instruments for measuring posttraumatic
stress disorder. Review Of Psychology, 10(1),
11-21.

Lyons, I. A., Caddell, I. M., Pittman, R. L., Rawls, R., &
Perrin, S. (1994). The potential for faking on the
Mississippi Scale for Combat-Related
PTSD. *Journal of Traumatic Stress,* 7,441-445.